UNSURPASSED

best wishes

Godfrey Barker

UNSURPASSED

THE STORY OF TOMMY GODWIN

THE WORLD'S GREATEST DISTANCE CYCLIST

Researched and told by a fellow club member at the

Stone Wheelers Cycling Club

GODFREY BARLOW

UNSURPASSED

First published in 2012 by Mousehold Press
www.mousehold-press.co.uk
for
Godfrey Barlow
Heath View, Sound Heath
Nantwich, CW5 8BD
www.stone-wheelers.co.uk

ISBN 978 1 874739 62 3

All profits from the sale of this book will be donated to
RoadPeace – the national charity for road crash victims.

CONTENTS

He was born in 1934 in North Staffordshire and was resident there until 1960. In this period he became a very keen racing cyclist becoming his club's, the North Staffs area, and the Manchester and District champion. This was along with over 120 outright victories and top ten finishes in a variety of events. He has been resident in South Cheshire for over 50 years, but still keeps in touch with his original cycling club: Stone Wheelers. In 2010 he was made a life member of his club and is also a member of the Fellowship of Cycling Old-Timers.

AUTHORS ACKNOWLEDGEMENTS:

Without the help of many people this book could not have been written.

A special thank you goes to the Stone Wheelers Cycling Club and members John Thornhill, Ray Hill and Paul Jennings for sponsoring the publication of this book.

Also thank you to Ivan Dix, Barbara Ford, Phil Dorman, Chris Watts, Jimmy Ogden, Dave Rodd and other members of Stone Wheelers Cycling Club for their contributions. Also a thank you to the Staffordshire Sentinel News and Media, the Archive department of Hanley, Stoke-on-Trent Library, Dr. Andrew Millward, Editor of the Fellowship News, The Black Anfielders and Adrian Bell for his valued advice. To all the other people I have missed out, my sincere apologies but thank you for your help.

I owe a debt to my wife Audrey for the time I have spent neglecting her while I was researching and writing and preparing this book. Also I dedicate this book to the memory of my late cycling friend Peter Clarke, who sadly died midway through my writing it.

PICTURE CREDITS:

Apologies for any poor quality pictures, as most are over 70 years old. I would like to thank *Cycling Weekly* for allowing a number of their images to be shown in this book (indicated *CW*). Other pictures are from Stone Wheelers archives, John Thornhill, Arthur Stubbs, Dave Rodd (indicated *DR*) and some from the author's own collection. A special thank you goes to Neil Hemmings for the loan of Tommy's Scrap Book and Diaries.

FOREWORD

I write as one of the privileged few people remaining who retain their own personal memories of Tommy Godwin. I started my cycling in Yorkshire, with Bronte Wheelers, but when work brought me to Stoke on Trent in 1950, as a graduate engineering assistant in the surveying department, I became a member of Stone Wheelers. Being in digs in Riverside Road, Trent Vale, I was a close neighbour of Tommy, his wife Betty and their family. Theirs was the first television I ever watched. Now at last his wonderful achievements have been lovingly researched, chronicled and published thanks to Godfrey Barlow.

Tommy always lived for the present, which, when I knew him best, was for the Stone Wheelers and its members. Before leaving to do my National Service in the Canal Zone in 1953, I was part of the Stone Wheelers story. Together with Ken Biddulph, John and Eric Thornhill we fielded formidable teams at all distances, winning notable events, including The Isle of Man mountain time trial and the Westerley Road Club, The Anfield and the Manchester Wheelers 100-mile events. Behind every success was Tommy.

In the early 1950s no one had ever beaten 58 minutes for a '25' and no one from any club in the Potteries had beaten 'the hour'. In 1952 Tommy told me that as long as I rode the Anfield '100' on Whit Monday, he would support me in the Solihull invitation '25' on the Sunday. We rode down to stay at the then famous 'Jack Simpsons Hostelry' on the Saturday. My 58.21 next morning proved to be a club and area record and afterwards Tommy and I rode up to Shrewsbury for the Anfield '100'. In those days it was a scenic course, the first leg going almost to Church Stretton, then back to Shrewsbury and on to Llanymynech, then up the Tanat valley, returning to finish in Shrewsbury. So, next morning, John and I backed up Eric for a team win, Eric being place fourth. I think Tommy was quietly satisfied with 'his boys' that Whit week-end.

I have met some of the pre-war record breakers referred to in this book; in particular Walter Greaves when he had his bike shop in Bradford and Bert James, who supplied us with four-speed Sturmey-Archer gears built into sprints! Sadly many of them will now have been forgotten but, thanks to Godfrey, Tommy never will be.

Jim Ogden
President 2005-2009, Veterans Time Trials Association
November 2011

PREFACE

This is a true story about a cycling challenge that was set up over one hundred years ago and of a rider who attempted it in 1939 and set the standard so high that his record remains unsurpassed after over seventy years. He has become the 'Greatest Long Distance Cyclist in the World'.

The challenge was simple to describe: it was to see who could ride a bicycle the greatest distance in a calendar year under the guidelines and monitoring of a cycling journal. This story follows the inception of this challenge and all who attempted it, and how it eventually turned into a test of human strength, stamina and endurance, which matches or exceeds most feats of endurance claimed by many sports people over this period of time. The publication includes the sporting life story of the man who put the record so far out of reach that no one has beaten it and maybe no one ever will.

What do we mean by endurance? Let's be specific and call it human endurance, where it is one person battling against the terrain, the elements, time, distance or whatever. Examples of these are: running an ultra or consecutive marathons, swimming across channels or seas, climbing an unclimbed mountain, trekking to the North or South Pole, rowing around the world and cycling across continents. When someone has achieved a recognised feat of endurance and it is witnessed and scrutinised fully, it usually gets great publicity, sometimes a book, TV programme or a film. Also it immediately sets a thought process in someone's mind to better that feat and in the next few years we usually hear of it being equalled or surpassed.

The man in this story is a 27 year old cyclist, born in Stoke-on-Trent, England, who started his challenge on January 1, 1939 and battled with the elements of a very severe British winter. During the year he had to deal with snow, ice, hail, wind, rain, a hot summer and mixed road conditions. He also had to deal with his personal demons, cuts and bruises after many falls, especially on ice, and then the outbreak of a World War with all its restrictions. He also had to confront another challenger who started at the same time and who, at times, matched and occasionally bettered his daily efforts.

Riding a bicycle can be fun. Many cyclists can do a trip of 30, 40 or even 50 miles in a day without it leaving any after effects. The more regularly you ride the easier it gets. Even for a fit rider, covering 100 to 150 miles in a day can leave them a little tired the following day and not wishing to do it again for a day or two.

Some ways of appreciating this man's achievement is to say that he cycled around the world four times in a year, or that he cycled from Lands End to John O'Groats eighty-eight times in a year! He achieved the unbelievable total of over 75,000 miles in the year by riding every single day, with exception of one day in the month of October just after he had beaten the previous record. His daily average for the 365 days was over 205 miles (329km). For many days he was riding for up to 18 hours at a time. Not satisfied with this remarkable feat he continued to ride until he completed 100.000 miles by Whitsun the following year.

Unfortunately for him World War II prevented the celebrity type follow-ups that record breakers usually receive.

Who is this man? He is Thomas Edward Godwin, known as Tommy. By some unfortunate fate there were two Tommy Godwin racing cyclists in roughly the same area and era.

This story concentrates on the endurance cyclist born in Fenton, Stoke-on-Trent in the year 1912. He often gets confused with another Tommy Godwin who was born in the USA in 1921 and who lived in the Birmingham area of England most of his long life. He became a track cyclist of repute and then a track cycling coach and owned a cycle shop in Birmingham. Having the same name, living in a roughly similar area of England and becoming famous in two very different areas in the sport of cycling, it is not surprising that the two are often confused.

One simple way of differentiating the two is to refer to the Stoke-on-Trent Tommy as the endurance one born in 1912, and refer to the other Tommy as the track rider and coach born in 1921.

The most remarkable fact of the two endurance records Tommy from Stoke-on-Trent established is that even after over 70 years have passed they still stand and have never been beaten. Looking back over this same period, how many other feats of human endurance have been achieved and then never equalled or bettered? Not many I would suspect. Surely this must be one of the most remarkable feats of human endurance ever undertaken?

On twenty days in an eight week period in the middle of 1939 he rode over 300 miles (482 km) in the day and never dropped his daily distance below 200 miles in this same period. It sounds unbelievable, but it is a true and it took place without the modern and lighter equipment, nutritional supplements and clothing that is available today.

As Tommy Godwin the endurance rider achieved these remarkable feats over 70 years ago, why write a story about him now?

Firstly, as the years have gone by and no cyclist has ever got anywhere near the magnitude of his endurance rides, his performance becomes more outstanding. Secondly, many people have asked the question as to why no book has ever been written about him. Somebody, in fact, asked this question in the *Fellowship News*, the quarterly magazine of the Fellowship of Cycling Old-Timers. As I knew Tommy personally and had kept many articles written about him in the local press, I could not resist the temptation to reply. Over a period I have sent a series of brief contributions to this magazine, which they have kindly published, and I have received many favourable comments about his story from as far afield as the USA. This book is a compilation and expansion of these contributions; I hope you enjoy them.

1

THE MAN I KNEW

It was 1949 and I was attending the Burslem Junior Technical School in Stoke-on-Trent, a type of higher education school for boys, and was riding my bicycle 9 miles each way to and from my home in Blurton. There was a boy in my class, Dave Hadley, who also rode his bicycle to school but who came in from another direction. We both joined the YHA (Youth Hostel Association) and later in the year went on a hostelling holiday to Cornwall together.

Cycling was something that I seemed to enjoy the more I did it. A friend, Graham Smith, who lived quite close to me and was attending the same school, suggested that we join a cycling club. He told me that a Ramon Hill, who was also attending the school, had joined the Stone Wheelers Cycling Club which had a clubroom in Stoke and he said it was the best club to join in the area. So we accepted this advice and both visited the clubroom. By 1950 we had both become junior members.

The club was certainly popular as there were regularly 25 to 30 members attending the clubroom on a Tuesday evening and even more turning out on the Sunday club runs. It took a while to get to know everybody, but one senior member seemed to stand out as most of the other senior members appeared to look up to him. Also on club nights the racing members of the club were always in discussion with him. As I later found out his name was Tommy Godwin and he was always encouraging the racing section of the club and organising, with other club members, support for the riders in the distance events by feeding and handing up drinks. I gradually got to know him and found him to be a very modest person who never spoke about his racing career. He was just under 40 years old then and had weather beaten features and was a very strong rider out on the club runs. He always preferred others to tell his tale. It must have been well over 12 months after joining the club that other club members started to tell me tales about Tommy's previous racing history.

What a history and what a tale. Most cyclists have achieved a big mileage in one day. Some are proud to have ridden 60 or 70 miles. Some regularly ride a 100 miles in a day. Competing cyclists in 12-hour time trials achieved mileages of 230 to around 280 miles in that period. Not many do the same the next day or in the following week. Even today riders at the top of their profession in events such as the Tour de France seldom ride stages longer than 150 miles (241km) in a day. Very few cyclists ride 200 miles a day for five consecutive days.

Tommy not only did this, but cycled an average of 200 miles a day for 500 days, yes five hundred days, completing the staggering total of 100,000 miles. This world record, together with his twelve months' total of 75,065 miles in 1939 has never been broken. He was the first and only cyclist ever to average over 200 miles a day for a twelve month period. As a teenager and not yet fully conversant with all the aspects of competitive cycle racing and riders' capabilities, these statistics of Tommy's records didn't mean a great deal to me then. The fact that he was a record holder meant more and I respected him for that fact alone. Over the many years since then, Tommy's record statistics have become more and more amazing, especially as the records still stand in the 21st Century.

Back to the Tommy I knew as manager and coach of Stone Wheelers Cycling Club. He was a very serious but cheerful character, always ready to give help and support to any club member, although he always expected you to respond to his demands and encouragement.

Club member John Thornhill, who joined Stone Wheelers Cycling Club before I did and is now the club's joint President with his wife Rae, told me about a training weekend he and his elder brother, Eric, had with Tommy around the year 1950. They had arranged to meet Tommy at his home in Trent Vale at 2.30pm on a Saturday. They found him finishing off decorating his living room - this after doing a night shift at the Tyre Company where he worked. They were soon on their way. Tommy's idea was that they ride through the night, but at about 3am the brothers insisted they stopped for rest and a few hours sleep. This they did under a hedge. Later Tommy went off to 'find' some breakfast and returned with a dozen eggs, which they cracked open and swallowed raw. After this they were quickly on their way and arrived at Lulworth Cove in Dorset at about 6am. The brothers soon realised this was a favourite spot for Tommy as he had occasionally stopped here during his record attempt. When they eventually arrived back at Tommy's home, he told them, "Not bad, but must do better next time". This was a round trip of around 500 miles.

* * * * *

In 1955 I resumed cycle racing after missing a year due to National Service commitments. Tommy then encouraged me to ride longer distances. Through bitter experience Tommy knew what it meant for riders to be 'looked after' in long distance events. He supported and motivated all club members when they entered these distance events. Together with his long term friends George and Edie Hemmings and other club members they would provide food, drink and motivation at all the strategic points on 100-mile and 12-hour time trials. When riders were riding events in other parts of the country, he would often ride out and be on hand to help and motivate them.

In June 1955 Tommy and other club members had supported me in my first open 100 mile time trial, the Abbotsford Park Road Club event, on mainly Cheshire roads. Tommy then suggested that I ride a 12-hour event, and the Oldbury and District Cycling Club 12-hour in mid September was the chosen event. He then suggested that to get used to riding for 12 hours, I ride the club place-to-place event, Stoke to Banbury and back a fortnight before. This was a distance of 172 miles. As we all thought this was a good idea the record attempt was set up. Marshalls and helpers were arranged and all went off successfully. After the Oldbury event Tommy had steered me into becoming the Stone Wheelers and the NCU (National Cycling Union) North Staffs Centre Best All-rounder champion of that year.

One vivid memory I still have of Tommy was seeing him suddenly appear in the road in front of me, jumping up and down, and shouting

Stone Wheelers Clubroom 1953
Back row (centre) Tommy Godwin, middle row (left) George Hemmings
and (centre) author, second row (left) John Thornhill.

Stone Wheelers Annual Club Dinner 1957. Club team members.
Left to right, Arthur Stubbs, author, Norman Guntripp
with a collection of trophies won during the year.

encouragement and to "put the hammer down" – a favourite phrase of his. This event was the well established classic Bath Road 100-mile time trial in 1956, the year when the Nottingham rider, Ray Booty of Ericsson Wheelers, broke the four hour barrier for the first time in a time trial of that distance. I had been riding well, in fact I was timed at the 71 mile checkpoint as lying in tenth place overall, in a star studded field of 100 riders, including such riders as Vin Denson, Bill Bradley, Stan Brittian, Billy Holmes, Owen Blower, Jimmy Ogden and many others. Unfortunately, between that checkpoint and where Tommy was positioned at the 75 mile point, I blew; it felt as if my leg muscles had deflated. I was spent, and no way could I respond to Tommy's encouragement. Tommy had ridden down especially to give me help where he thought I needed it most. He was right, but I was in no position to respond and felt I had let him down badly.

The following week I can remember riding the Broad Oak CC 12-hour event that covered roads in and around Nottinghamshire, when he linked up with my father to look after me as the event was too far away to expect the usual club members' support. Although I only finished in 8th position, Tommy had encouraged me to do my personal best distance and he had steered me to win both Best All-rounder competitions again.

The following year, 1957, Tommy encouraged me on to even greater things. By breaking club records for a 100-mile and 12-hour time trial, I was able to add the new Manchester & District Time Trials Association Best All-rounder title to the other two I gained. But the Manchester Wheelers 12-hour event I rode was a near disaster. The course, after covering many out and back journeys around Cheshire and Shropshire, finished on a circuit of eleven miles at the 210 mile point. After one lap of the circuit I felt very tired. Choosing a quiet stretch of road with a wide verge and fairly soft hedge, I decided to have a rest by leaning on it and closed my eyes. After a short time I was rudely awoken by Tommy telling me to get a move on and make sure that I finished with a decent mileage.

My bike was much lighter in weight than Tommy's had been on his record rides and I had the choice of ten gears against his four. It was much later in life that I realised that the distance I had completed in these infrequent 12-hour events was a normal distance that Tommy used to ride day after day, month after month.

One of the few comments he made about his ride to his clubmates was that he had started at the wrong time! A start a few months later would have meant that he would have had to endure only one bad winter, not the two severe ones that he suffered.

2

TOMMY'S EARLY YEARS

Tommy was born June 5, 1912 in Fenton, Stoke-on-Trent, the eldest son of a family, of 10 children. He had a very tough upbringing as World War I ('The War to End All Wars') started when he was only two years of age. Tommy started earning for his family around the age of twelve, delivering orders for the proprietor of a general store, butcher and newsagents. He used a heavy 'shop bike'- they now appear to be called cargo bikes – complete with carrier and basket on the front. He thoroughly enjoyed riding this bike and it is reliably documented that when aged fourteen years old he spotted a poster advertising for riders for a local 25-mile cycle time trial. Tommy entered this event, his first ever race. With the help of his employer and a friend they helped him strip the delivery bike down and took off whatever they could, including the front carrier. Hearsay has it that with a pair of borrowed wheels and shoes he rode the shop bike in the time trial and won the event in a time of sixty-five minutes. Whatever the facts were, one thing that was certain is that Tommy enjoyed competing and thought that this was to be the ideal sport for him.

He then joined the Potteries Clarion Cycling Club, later the North Staffordshire Cycling Club, then settled in with what was the premier North Staffs cycling club at that time, the Potteries Cycling Club. With this latter club he became one of the fastest 25-mile and 50-mile time trialers in the country, when on no fewer than four occasions he achieved times of less than 1 hour 2 minutes at a time when riding a 25-mile time trial in less than sixty minutes was completely unheard of.

At the other end of the scale he had covered 236 miles in a 12-hour time trial. In the early 1930s he was a member of a very successful Potteries CC team when, with F. T. 'Freddie' Brown and others, they won many team prizes in distance events, including the famous Bath Road 100-mile event and in many shorter events.

In 1933 Tommy was very pleased to have finished in 7th position in the recently formed Best All-rounder Competition. This was a competition held over 50 and 100 miles and 12-hour time trials, and open to all amateur cyclists in Great Britain. A list was drawn up with riders' times and distance for the said events and then at the end of the season an average speed was worked out. His times for that year were: for a 50-mile event 2 hours 10 minutes and 12 seconds; for a 100-mile event 4 hours 40 minutes and 6 seconds; and for the 12-hour event his distance was 231 5/8 miles. This worked out at an average speed of 21.255 miles per hour.

Also in the same year he was a member of the Potteries CC team that won a team award in the classic Anfield Bicycle Club's 100-mile time trial. He treasured that prize because it was won on his actual birthday that year. This annual event is still held to this day. The Anfield club was founded in Liverpool in 1879, which was indeed before the Liverpool Football club was established there; it was a club with many famous achievements and promoted many events. The most famous one was their annual 100-mile time trial first held in 1889 as a paced event. As it became popular, problems arose as to the number of competitors and helpers who were crowding the roads and people started to complain. A change had to be made. It startled many competitors when the start time was changed by the organisers to 4.30 am, the idea being that the race could be completed before the local policemen had finished their breakfast.

From 1900 it became an unpaced event held at Whitsun time on roads around Shrewsbury. Tommy rode this event many times but never won it.

In the 1930s and 1940s bike equipment was quite heavy, especially compared with the super lightweight equipment and bike frames available today. The same went for cycle clothing; many clothes were made of wool which soaked up water. Riding in the rain just made the clothes heavier. Tyres certainly were not puncture proof and punctures were very common.

Around 1936 Tommy was finding work difficult to find in the Potteries. He later moved down to London and found work with a bicycle builder in Northwood Hills in the North-West London area, between Harrow and Rickmansworth, and he joined the Rickmansworth Cycling Club. This was a well established club having been founded in 1901. He continued with his achievements, including in 1938 winning for his new club the Vegetarian Cycling & Athletic Club's 50-mile time trial in a time of 2 hours 8 minutes and 25 seconds, in a top class field of riders. Also he finished in second position in the Polytechnic Cycling Club 12-hour event. Tommy had many friends in the Vegetarian C & AC and he became associated with it as with many other clubs, including the Birchfield Cycling & Athletic Club.

Over this time period Tommy had amassed a staggering total of 200 medals, trophies and awards. About fifty of these he treasured dearly as they had a very special meaning to him. But riding as an amateur there was little to be gained in providing for the necessities of life.

The advert that started it all, distributed by *Cycling* in 1910 to announce the first 'year-long' competition. *DR*

3

HOW IT ALL STARTED

Let us take a look at how the year's distance record was started and the riders who have challenged and increased the distance of this record over the years.

It was at the beginning of the twentieth century and the British automotive industry was in its infancy. Cycling was the more popular method of mechanical transport and recreation as motor cars were not yet a familiar sight on the roads, but there were plenty of horse drawn vehicles. A lot of cyclists were covering many miles and all the world and his wife were claiming that they had covered more miles in a year than anybody else.

After dealing with multitudes of non-validated claims for the highest mileages recorded for this one-year period, the *Cycling* magazine decided in 1910 to announce a verified competition for this achievement entitled *Cycling's Century Competition* for the year 1911. Originally the idea of the competition was to verify the number of times in a year a rider had completed a 100-mile ride. It developed quickly into a competition to see how many total miles a rider had ridden in a one year period. Part of the verification process was for the rider to post in to the magazine a daily checking card completed for each day's ride with the start point, finishing point and total day's distance witnessed by a local official such as a Postmaster, Council Official, Policeman, Clergyman, Nurse or such person.

Cycling is one of the oldest cycling magazines published. It has had various slight changes to its published title and is still produced today under the title of *Cycling Weekly*.

The first cyclist to enter this challenge was a French man, Marcel Planes. In 1911 he claimed the inaugural verified distance record of

34,366 miles (55,305 km). *Cycling* accepted this claim as Marcel had complied with their verification system. The cycling world in general also appeared to accept this claim as a remarkable feat, as he averaged nearly 100 miles every day.

Not a lot seems to be known about him except for the fact he was always seen to appear and be one of the first people to congratulate succeeding riders who attempted or broke this distance record.

After Marcel's inaugural distance record ride in 1911, the years ticked by. The 1914-1918 World War was started and was finished. Many people had their minds on other important things, such as getting their lives together after that brutal war. Nobody seemed interested in a challenge to Marcel's record distance. At that time not many cyclists would contemplate devoting a whole year to attack Marcel's record and it seemed that the record distance might stay in the record books for ever.

Then out of the blue, 21 years later, an Englishman plucked up the courage and wanted to show what an ordinary clubman could achieve on an ordinary clubman's bicycle. This was Arthur Humbles, a 22-year-old member of the Ingleside Cycling Club. He set out on January 8, 1932 to try to improve on Marcel's bench mark distance. He averaged throughout the year just a fraction over 100 miles a day. His longest ride on any one day was 172 miles. Most of his rides were from London, out and back along on the Great North Road, the Cambridge Road and the Newmarket Road.

These were not the only routes undertaken as he toured England and Wales for considerable periods, recording visits to places as far apart as Alnwick, Clovelly, Bury St. Edmunds and Bere Regis.

He broke Marcel's previous record on December 11, 1932 by riding at the head of a gigantic club run from Buckingham Palace, through Hyde Park to Marble Arch in London. He was cheered on by many cyclists ringing their bicycle bells, with many other onlookers cheering. He had caught the public's attention with his exploit. As he passed the previous record, which had stood for 21 years, he received an accolade from no less a person than Sir Malcolm Campbell, the world land and water speed record holder.

On presenting him with a silver trophy and a laurel wreath, he is reported to have said, "Your great effort in creating this new record for Britain reflects great credit on the grit and determination of a young man, who, finding himself unemployed, thought out this means of doing good, both for himself and for the British cycling industry."

Humbles continued to ride, adding over 1,600 more miles and by December 31, 1932 he had completed a total of 36,007 miles (57,946 km) to establish a new world record for riding a bicycle for a whole year.

Arthur Humbles had the distinction of becoming one of the first entries in the *Golden Book of Cycling*, which was an equivalent to a 'Hall of Fame' used by many sporting bodies and was created by the *Cycling* magazine in 1932. The purpose of this *Golden Book* was to celebrate the sport and pastime of cycling by recording the outstanding rides, deeds and accomplishments of cyclists, officials and administrators. Each page was crafted to honour a single hero. The original book was finished in 1972, but the tradition has been continued by The Pedal Club.

This club was founded in 1941 by a group of cycling journalists and officials wishing to meet and exchange diverse views. In 1946 the membership was broadened to include those who have rendered service to cycling. They met regularly at their Headquarters, The Prince of Wales pub-restaurant, Drury Lane, Covent Garden in London.

Arthur received good world-wide press coverage for his record ride. This made many people aware of his attack on the world record, including Tommy and an Australian rider by the name of Oserick Bernard Nicholson, known as 'Ossie'. He was born in Tasmania in 1906 and when he was a teenager his family moved to Victoria, which is the smallest of the mainland states in Australia. He worked as a blacksmith near his home in a suburb of Melbourne. He was short in stature but powerfully built and was known as the 'pocket Hercules'.

Ossie joined a cycling club and showed such natural speed that he was encouraged to enter in club races. After winning a few races he became a professional rider at the age of 22. He then went on to win several professional road races, some controversially. He also rode and won many track races including motor- paced events on the Melbourne track. He had many brushes with officialdom and was suspended once for three months. One rider, who Ossie competed against regularly, was one of Australia's greatest ever cyclists, Hubert 'Oppy' Opperman who was a professional with the *Malvern Star* cycling team. Eventually Ossie joined this team. Oppy later became Sir Hubert Opperman and a member of the Australian government.

While Arthur Humbles was setting his new record in 1932, it was well reported in Australia. The manager of *Malvern Star*, Bruce Small, thought that getting an Australian rider to break this record would be a great publicity stunt for the company. He approached several riders, including Opperman, who all refused. Happy-go-lucky Ossie agreed as he was always up for a new challenge. Then it was all systems go in preparation for it. His tyres were to be supplied by Dunlop and his gears by Cyclo. This was to be a Cyclo 3-speed derailleur gear which was the first of its type available in Australia and had only been introduced there a few months previously.

So, twenty-six years old Ossie Nicholson set out on January 1, 1933 to begin his challenge to this one day old record ride set by Arthur Humbles the day before at 36,007 miles (57,946 km).

He was limited in the choice of routes he could take as Australia being such a vast country, the distance between towns and cities was huge. A circuit around the Melbourne area was used often, but he felt he needed to vary the routes to relieve boredom. Then, when he travelled outside Melbourne he would travel for miles without meeting a living soul. Ossie also found the summer heat exhausting, leaving him very tired and a single night's rest was not enough to wipe out every nuance of exhaustion. He relied heavily on his trainer giving him daily massage and advising him as to what and when to eat to give him the correct level of nutrition.

His sponsors needed him to appear at public functions, and with all the publicity he became a national figure with many people recognising him as he rode through populated areas. By October 31, 1933 he had beaten Arthur Humble's record. As a publicity stunt his sponsors arranged for him to ride through a paper screen erected outside their headquarters.

Ossie was determined to set an unbeatable record by riding a minimum of 100 miles every day. Near the end of his ride, when somebody suggested that someone could beat this by riding in a leap year, Ossie responded by riding over 200 miles on the last day of the year, which, of course, was a summer day down-under. He ended the year averaging 120 miles a day, recording a total of 43,966 miles (70,756 km), the new world record. As Ossie had complied with the *Cycling* verification system his claim was accepted.

The fact that this record had been broken in two consecutive years began to create even more interest in the cycling community. But nobody had the courage to take up the challenge to Ossie's record for three years. Then, in 1936, along came a controversial character from Yorkshire determined to break the Australian's record. He was a member of the Vegetarian Cycling and Athletic Club named Walter Greaves.

Walter, who was born in 1907, had lost his left forearm in an accident whilst a young teenager. He wanted to compete with normal two-armed people and had some measure of success in the sports of rugby and running. He joined a cycling club in 1932 and raced creditably at all distances on the road, sometimes competing with Tommy. Walter was, like Tommy, a vegetarian and also teetotal, as a reaction to having an alcoholic father. He was an engineer by trade, but his communist politics and troublemaking personality made it very difficult for him to get work. In 1935 he had the idea of challenging the year distance record, especially as the following year was a leap year, giving him an extra day's riding. He appealed to the cycle industry for sponsorship without success.

Eventually a small bike shop 'Three Spires Cycles' agreed to sponsor him. They said they would provide a bicycle for the start on January 1, 1936 and help him in other ways financially. This meant that he would start the challenge as a professional. He was pleased at this offer and set about preparing himself in the other necessary ways. When the New Year arrived, Walter's promised bike didn't. When it eventually did arrive, Walter lost more time having it adapted to his one-armed riding style. This meant having his one-sided handlebar equipped with a single brake lever that was coupled to both front and rear brakes and a twist grip gear changer on this single handlebar as well. Also a rest was fitted on the left side for his stump. The gears that were fitted gave him a choice of 59, 71 and 79 inches. (For an explanation of how they are calculated see Chapter 4.)

Walter commenced his ride on January 6, from Bradford five days later than planned with the target of 43,996 miles to beat. The first day he set out to ride to York and back, and in four of the first seven days he was soaked by rain. Soon snow and ice appeared and one day, riding through the North Yorkshire moors, he was reported to have fallen eight times. It was a severe winter and he had many other falls. Despite the bad weather Walter was averaging 120 miles a day, which was his minimum target. He had to have his handlebar modified again, this time to have a new cup fitted to accommodate his stump in a more comfortable way than the one he had originally fitted, which was causing some discomfort.

Soon he was going further afield and finding better weather and by mid-June he had completed 21,500 miles (34,600 km), which meant that he was on course to break Ossie Nicholson's record. Then a small hiccup occurred that led to a bigger problem. A collision with a car near Stockton-on-Tees in July damaged his leg and then an abscess formed on it, which in turn caused blood poisoning. He was off his saddle for thirteen days while he had an operation and treatment in hospital. He then had to reset his daily target to make up for lost time.

Walter managed to get back on his target and passed Nicholson's figure of 43,996 miles on December 13, 1936 with nearly three weeks of the year still left. Again it was celebrated with a giant club run of cyclists through Hyde Park. As a nation we have always enjoyed beating the Australians at whatever!

He went on to amass a total of 45,383 miles (73,037 km) for the year, finishing his ride outside Bradford Town Hall at midnight on New Year's Eve before a huge crowd of well-wishers. His highest distance in one day had been 262 miles, but he did ride 374 miles in one stretch over two days without sleep to help him get back onto his schedule after his unfortunate delays. It follows that his year, instead of having the planned 366 days of riding, had only 348 days riding after his two major problems. This gave Walter an average of 130 miles for each riding day. He always said that if it wasn't for the abscess on his leg he could have completed 50,000 miles for the year.

Walter complied with the *Cycling* verification process and his claim was accepted. He also had the honour of an entry in the *Golden Book of Cycling* and included in it was the following: "By this great performance, Greaves not only brought the record back to England but demonstrated the ease of cycling in all weathers and in everyday traffic conditions, even for a man thus handicapped.

Furthermore, he finished the ride a bronzed, healthy and fit man in splendid contrast to the out-of-work, sickly and pale person who twelve months previously possessed little more than the courage to tackle the big task he carried through to its successful conclusion."

Walter had the good fortune to be reinstated as an amateur racing cyclist. This was not an easy objective to achieve, but the governing body thought that Walter's case needed special consideration. He then used his engineering skills and went on to manufacture bicycles. He fell out with the Vegetarian C&AC and with a friend, Geoff Wood, formed the Airedale Olympic Road Club, which became one of the early clubs affiliated to the BLRC (British League of Racing Cyclists founded in 1942).

During Walter's ride the interest in this endurance test increased beyond belief. The fact that he had beaten Ossie Nicholson's 'unbeatable' total, despite his late start, being nearly a fortnight incapacitated and riding with only one arm, was truly incredible. It follows that whatever Walter ended up with as a total, it had to be beatable.

Three riders made it clear during Walter's ride that as soon as he finished on December 31, 1936 they were going to challenge it from the next day. Who were these riders? First was the Australian professional Ossie Nicholson, who wanted to regain the record back for himself and Australia. Secondly, an English amateur cyclist Bernard Bennett from Birmingham who said he was going to ride the challenge just for fun and third, René Menzies, a 48 year old Frenchman (of Scottish decent) who was living in England and sponsored by a British cycle manufacturer – Rudge-Whitworth.

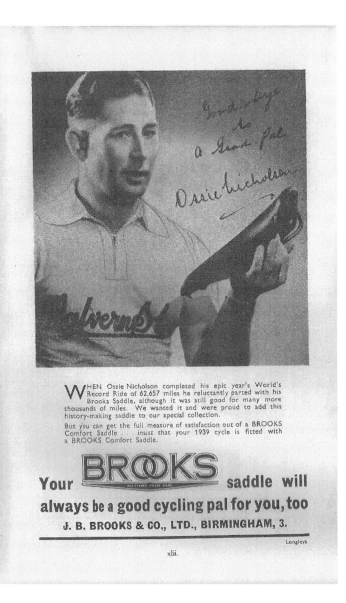
Brooks saddles are still a favourite with many cyclists today. *DR*

So on January 1, 1937 Ossie started out, about 10 kilograms overweight, but with reasonable weather in Australia was recording about 186 miles (300 km) a day and in the heat of the summer he soon regained his racing weight. He had a few problems and had to take several days off due to sunstroke, a poisoned toe and tonsillitis, but he pressed on strongly. At the end of May he had recorded 24,840 miles (40,000 km). As it was now nearing wintertime in Australia Ossie's daily mileage began to reduce. René Menzies, who had been handicapped with colder weather from the start, began to close the gap that Ossie had created by using the longer days available to ride roads in the UK and in Europe. Ossie responded by riding in the dark and by the start of October they were riding neck and neck although many continents apart.

Rene had some bad luck when, after a crash, he broke a bone in his wrist and rode for weeks with the wrist in plaster and a sling. Both riders passed Walter Greaves' record of 45,383 miles (73,037 km) on the same day. But as winter began to set in for René, Ossie, with the better weather, moved ahead and finished the year 1,096 miles (1,763 km) ahead of him. Their respective final distances were Ossie with 62,657 miles (100,837 km) and René with 61,561 miles (99,073 km).

Meanwhile, Bernard Bennett set a new amateur record with 45,801 miles (73,710 km), which also beat Walter Greaves' record by just 418 miles (673 km). René Menzies continued to ride daily and set a new record for riding 100,000 miles in 532 days. After Ossie's new record nobody was waiting to challenge it in 1938.

Menzies had been decorated with the Croix de Guerre in the First World War. In the Second World War he became a chauffeur to the French Leader, General Charles de Gaulle. He spent a lot of his time in England and in 1952, to celebrate his 63rd birthday, he set out again to ride for a year with the object of riding 63,000 miles and beating Ossie Nicholson's record of 1937. He did not meet his first objective; he failed by 215 miles, but he did have the satisfaction of beating the Australian's total by 128 miles.

Elliman rub advert *circa* 1938. In the past it was used by many cyclists.
Today it is still available in many shops. *DR*

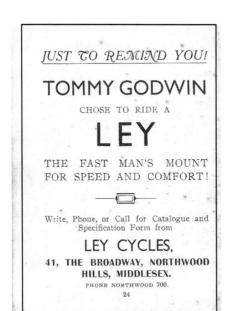

Tommy's original sponsor. The advert appeared in a cycling club handbook for 1939. *DR*

4

THE 1939 CHALLENGE

Tommy continued collecting awards in time trials across the country up to the end of the 1938 season. Although one of the fastest 25 and 50 milers in the country, he was now competing well in the distance events, he never seemed to be troubled by them and found that he was able to recover quite quickly. At the end of 1937 when the Australian, Ossie Nicholson, took the record off Walter Greaves, Tommy had an idea that he would like to get it back for Britain. He discussed this idea with several friends who said that if he did make an attempt on the year's record they would support him if at all possible.

Later Tommy discussed the idea with his employer, Mr. A.T. Ley, who after some deliberation, agreed to sponsor him for the attempt on the year mileage record. Plans were then drawn up for the start on New Year's Day 1939, his thirteenth racing season. First, Tommy had to change his status from an amateur cyclist to become a professional. This was done in November 1938 for the sole purpose of attacking the year's record. Changing status was a very important consideration to undertake at this period of time. The rules for amateurs were very strict: if a cyclist took any kind of financial reward, even expenses, he would be disqualified from competing in any more amateur events. To be able to carry on racing, the only option a rider had was to get someone to sponsor him and become a professional cyclist, which would give him with very little opportunity to race regularly again in the United Kingdom. After being a professional, the option to revert back to being an amateur was very seldom allowed by the governing body.

This specially sealed and tamper-proof speedometer is now fitted to Tommy's bike in preparation for the 1 January 1939 start.

Next Mr. Ley was to build Tommy a frame and then choose what equipment was to go on it. His frame was built with Reynolds 531 tubing and was to be named a 'Ley TG Special'. The top specification equipment chosen was a Baylis-Wiley (BW) bottom bracket, a Williams chain wheel and cranks, Brooks saddle, Dunlop 27 inch High Pressure wheels and tyres, Solite front hub, Resilian cantilever brakes, Bluemel lightweight mudguards and a Smiths speedometer. The decision on gears was deferred, but later a Sturmey-Archer 3 speed hub gear was decided on. This had been used by some of Tommy's friends in recent successful Road Record Association (RRA) record attempts. The first Sturmey-Archer 3 speed hub gear was launched at the Cycle Show in 1902, so Tommy was choosing reliability.

Also attacking the year's record were two more riders. The first was a previous amateur record holder for the event, Bernard Bennett from Birmingham, now riding as a professional with New Hudson Cycles. His equipment was to be a New Hudson Featherweight Club model equipped with a 3 speed Cyclo 'Oppy' Derailleur Gear and Dunlop Tyres. The model 'Oppy' was named after the great Australian cyclist, Sir Hubert Opperman, who came to Britain in 1934 and 1935 and broke many RRA place-to-place records using this gear. The second rider was another Englishman, amateur Edward Swann from London, an ex-member of the Actonia Cycling Club. His equipment was unknown.

New Year's day 1939 had arrived; 26 year old Tommy was physically and mentally prepared to start the attempt on the year distance record. His bike was ready, the specially sealed Smiths speedometer had been installed, he had a large supply of the *Cycling* daily checking cards and he was ready to start the challenge.

The previous night Tommy had invited two friends from the Potteries to stay with him at his lodgings in Great Elms Road, Nash Mills, Hemel Hempstead. James Carr and the other friend had cycled down by tandem with the idea of riding with him back to James's home in Hanley. James was a long term friend of Tommy's and was a member of the famous Anfield Bicycle Club. James, as well as being a friend, was looked up to by Tommy and advised him on many things connected with cycling. James had the distinction of winning his club's prestigious 100-mile time trial in 1935 and their now lapsed 12-hour event in 1934 and 1937.

The two friends were up early in the morning and were surprised to find Tommy was out. He then returned with the news that he started out about 5am when it was raining heavily, but had already put 82 miles on his newly installed tamper proof speedometer.

The official send-off was outside his sponsor's (Ley Cycles) cycle shop premises, 41, The Broadway, Northwood Hills, Middlesex, just after noon on January 1, 1939. Tommy announced that if he was well ahead of schedule he would consider attacking a RRA record or two. Tommy was officially sent on his way by Capt. George Eyston, the well known racing motorist and holder of the world's land speed record, who gave Tommy some words of encouragement and wished him good luck. There was a large crowd present and the local policeman wrongly suspected a riot and called for back-up. The crowd included about 200 cyclists; his current club the Rickmansworth Cycling Club was well represented along with many other cycling clubs from the area. Also present was a lady record-breaking cyclist and tricyclist 'Billie' Dovey, who pinned a twig of heather to him for luck. She had just finished riding her bicycle for a full year (1938) in demonstrating 'Fitness for Women' and completed 29,604 miles (47,641 km). This event propelled her into the media limelight and she featured on a set of Players cigarette cards in 1939. She knew Tommy quite well as they often competed in similar distance cycle events.

Tommy was wearing tights and a heavy sweater as the temperature had been little above freezing point when he'd set out earlier. The weather had now improved and the sun was shining when he set off, heading for Hanley (Stoke-on-Trent) about 150 miles away. His plan was simple; he set himself the task of riding 200 miles a day in four 'bursts' of 50 miles, taking time off for food and rest. The record holder, the Australian Ossie Nicholson, had averaged 172 miles a day in setting the current record of 62,657 miles (100,834 km).

It follows that Tommy had to average just 28 miles a day more to hit his target. How many readers will have ridden 28 miles today, yesterday and every day for a year? Also you have to remember this was on top of the 172 miles average each day that Tommy had to ride to equal the Australian's record.

As well as being teetotal he was a vegetarian, a decision he made in his early years after working for a Burslem (Stoke-on-Trent) pie maker. It obviously had a lifetime effect after he saw what was being put in these pies. His diet was basically milk (4 pints a day), eggs, cheese and bread. He would then add seasonable fruit and vegetables and chocolate to give a bit of variety. It was important that this endurance event would require very careful managing of food and drink input. If he wasn't careful and his energy needs were not balanced with his food intake, it could spell disaster for Tommy's target of beating the record.

As he got further north on this first day the weather worsened, but he reached Hanley that night without mishap. He was very pleased that he had completed well over his target of 200 miles for the day. After a night's rest at James Carr's house he was up early the following morning and set out north on his way into Lancashire. Tommy was back in the Potteries a few days later having run into severe weather in the Preston area. By now almost the whole country was snowbound with three foot snowdrifts followed by 18 degrees of frost. Tommy's friends in the Potteries then came to his rescue because they had been studying the weather charts, and had discovered there was a small belt of land comparatively free from snow and ice in the West Country. It was here that Tommy went, cycling up and down the same roads to keep up his mileage until the weather improved. Because of the bad winter weather he was not able to record another 200 miles plus day's ride until January 15.

Meanwhile Bernard Bennett had planned to start at one minute past midnight but bad weather delayed his start. He set out from his home in Birmingham on New Year's Day at 4 am with members of his family cheering him on his way. New Hudson had prepared an official send off at the Black Horse Hotel in Birmingham, where representatives of the cycle trade and many club cyclists had gathered. Mr. Horace Brueton, chairman of New Hudson gave him good wishes on behalf of the company. Cycle trade representatives included H.R. Horden of J.B. Brooks & Co Ltd, H. Ryan of Dunlop Rubber Co Ltd, Louis Camillis of Cyclo Gear Co Ltd and C. E. Pigg of Reynolds Tube Co. Ltd.

This is Tommy posting one of the hundreds of his witnessed checking cards to the scrutineers of his challenge.

Bernard's 1937 attempt was said to be 'just for fun', but this time he was deadly serious and spent a lot of time training for it. Bernard started with the intention of using his Birmingham home as a base for riding out and back routes and having a hot midday meal there every day. He also planned to start slowly and build up his mileage later in the year when the weather improved. Unfortunately his start turned out to be much slower than expected. There was a lot of snow around Birmingham that January and he suffered a lot. The weather was so bad that his highest mileage on four consecutive days in early January was only 65 miles, with one day not recording any mileage at all. On another day he lost several hours waiting for a replacement wheel, which had been damaged in a tumble on the icy roads. Another delay was when he was receiving medical treatment for a strained leg.

The other challenger, Edward Swann, started out from Cricklewood, North London at 4.30 am in drizzling rain. It wasn't a spectacular send-off as the only witness was a *Cycling* photographer. His aim was to ride to Bath and back and in the first week he twice had the misfortune to fall badly on icy roads, injuring his ankle and knee. He was ordered to rest and stated that he was determined to carry on with his challenge when he improved. He never did, and gracefully retired from the challenge with only 939 miles recorded.

But it was a bad winter that year, and on many a night when the wind was howling and the snow driving across the roads, Tommy was a solitary figure in sweater and woollen tights, pedalling along some lonely country road. Often he went cycling when no motorist would have dared go out. One terrible day, when all traffic had stopped because of snow and intense cold, Tommy fell off his machine about 20 times between Stone, Staffordshire and Hanley, Stoke-on Trent, but was still able to cover nearly 200 miles. Several times he rode through the night and spent the next day on the road as well. Snow, rain, hail and fog all combined to keep his mileage well behind schedule in the first two months of the year. On one occasion, at Bicester, a car collided with his machine and wrecked the rear wheel. Fortunately traffic was moving slowly at the time and he was not injured, although twice in this first month Tommy had to visit hospital due to his crashes and spills.

Tommy used a special version of this speedometer. It had only recently been introduced in 1937 and proved to be very accurate for mileage recording.

After 35 days into the ride Tommy was over 2,500 miles ahead of Bernard's total. But in the next five weeks or so there was still quite a lot of snow and this winter weather was making riding terribly hard, his average was dropping and his leg and other muscles hardened. He really thought that he would have to give up the attempt. He kept going with dogged determination and as the weather improved gradually his fitness returned.

After his very slow start Bernard Bennett had the good fortune to obtain the assistance of a helper and advisor, the legendary René Menzies, who had challenged Ossie Nicholson all the way in the record attempts in 1937, the same year that Bernard had set the amateur record of 45,801 miles (73,710 km). René had quite an impact on Bernard, who by early March was producing better daily and weekly distances than Tommy was. A significant day was March 9, when Bernard completed 263 miles, bettering Tommy's best daily total of 234 miles in January.

Another time, Tommy's daily mileage suffered because he had to have some teeth out. He was forced to waste time going to the dentist and the following day he felt too ill to do his normal high mileage.

His great friend and advisor James Carr, whose home in Hanley he made one of his unofficial headquarters, remembers Tommy's famous ride well. "Many a time Tommy turned up here completely exhausted and we had to bath him and put him to bed," he said. "Sometimes he was so wet that we had to take off his clothes and ring them out. The water poured from them." James was also Treasurer of a new North Staffs cycling club named 'Mercury Aces'. It was an offshoot of the North Staffs Cyclists Touring Club section and was designed to cater for the racing needs for some of its members. Sadly this new club did not survive for long; World War II killed it off.

One of the other unofficial headquarters was Tommy's digs in Nash Hills, Hemel Hempstead. He was lodging with a Mr Frank and Mrs Nellie Roome. They seemed to put up with his irregular appearances. As with his Hanley base he was often away for weeks at a time when he was cycling in other parts of England and Scotland. He gave Wales a wide berth, after trying one or two routes, because the hilly terrain upset his rhythm. To avoid boredom he varied his routes as much as possible. Inevitably some routes did get more used than others. From the Potteries he would often ride to Banbury and back, especially in the winter months when the weather was bad. It was not quite his daily target of 200 miles, but at over 170 miles it helped build up his total mileage.

Then, when based in the London area, he would use the Bath Road out of London to Bath and back and this would give him a useful mileage of over 210. He also used many other Home Counties routes. By March the weather gradually improved and so did Tommy's mileage. Later in that month he was persuaded by the Sturmey-Archer company to install their revolutionary new four speed AF hub giving him gear ratios of 57, 74, 86 and 97 inches.

These numbers are a curious survival of the days of the 'old ordinary' bicycle. They relate to the diameter of the wheel with a fixed pedal on it. Therefore, on bicycles as we know them today, a calculation has to be made with three factors: the number of teeth on the chain-wheel, the number of teeth on the rear sprocket and the diameter of the rear wheel in inches. On hub gears, like Tommy was using, one gear is direct drive and the others calculated as a percentage from it, worked out by the manufacturer. In Tommy's case his chain-wheel had 48 teeth, his rear sprocket had 15 teeth and his wheel diameter was 27 inches. This gave Tommy a gear size of 86 inches for the direct drive in his new four-speed hub gear, which applied to his third gear. The remaining gears are worked out using the Sturmey-Archer gear ratio tables to apply a factor to the direct drive gear to obtain the first, second and fourth gears.

Tommy was quickly able to take advantage of the extra gear, and with the improved weather was able to get his daily distances back to around the 200 mile target that he had set himself. On Tuesday March 28 he rode from Hemel Hempstead to Devizes and Chippenham, covering 205 miles. He rode 185 miles on the following day and then on the following Thursday he headed north to Birmingham, Shrewsbury, Newcastle-under-Lyme and Hanley for a distance of exactly 200 miles.

On April 21 he finally bettered Bernard's highest daily mileage riding 295 miles. Eight days later Bernard managed to better it by just one mile. He was gradually narrowing the lead that Tommy had built up in the early period of the attempt.

Tommy was suffering from saddle soreness, for which he obtained a special ointment. Then later, on the advice of a girl cyclist, he wore ladies' silk under garments. This could possibly have been either Pearl Wellington or Marguerite Wilson, two record distance cyclists who were supporting Tommy whenever they could.

As the month of May approached with much better weather, his initial sponsor was struggling to keep up with Tommy's demands. Also, with the threat of a world war looming, an alternative sponsor was sought by Tommy's friends and supporters. At this stage his total distance had increased to around 27,000 miles (43,451 km), but Bernard Bennett was steadily reducing Tommy's lead over him to around 960 miles (1,544 km).

The deal has been done. Officials of Tommy's new sponsors gather outside Winchester Cathedralfor his first day riding a Raleigh Record Ace.
27 May 1939.

Refreshments served by Charlie Davey while Tommy adjusts his bike. *CW*

5

RALEIGH TO THE RESCUE

The month of May was a decisive month for Tommy. He had overcome some of his earlier problems and by the middle of May he was at last regularly completing daily rides of 200 miles plus. Negotiations were taking place by Tommy's friends to find a new sponsor to replace Mr. Ley, and then it was found that the Raleigh Cycle Company was eager to do it. This challenge seemed a natural extension to the many place-to-place records the company had captured in the previous few years. After brief discussions and the necessary equipment obtained, an official launch was arranged to take place in Winchester on May 27, 1939. Raleigh officials gathered outside Winchester Cathedral to give Tommy a good send-off for his first day's ride as a Raleigh Cycles/Sturmey-Archer professional. He was now riding a standard Raleigh Record Ace racing bike, with Dunlop Sprite Tyres, Brooks B17 saddle and, of course, he continued with the new revolutionary Sturmey-Archer four speed medium-ratio hub gear and the Smiths speedometer. Sid Ferris, Charles Holland, and Bert James had all used this type of bike for achieving ten new RRA records in the previous two years, but with the three speed Sturmey-Archer hub gear.

He now had the support of Raleigh Cycles Team's well known coach, Charlie Davey, for whom Tommy had the greatest respect. In fact, he always addressed him as 'Mr. Davey', which was the formal way of addressing someone at that time. Charlie was a star distance performer in his own right. During his racing career he competed in the first World Championship Road Race for amateurs held in Copenhagen in 1921 and won a bronze medal. He repeated this achievement the following year when it was held in Shropshire, England with another bronze medal. The Anfield Bicycle Club organised this event on behalf of the national organisation. Charlie's club at that time was the Vegetarian Cycling and Athletic Club. In 1923 he embarked on a four year professional career and went on to break several Road Records Association (RRA) records. These records included the Land's End to London, London to Bath and back, London to Portsmouth and back and 24-hour records. In 1929 he helped to re-launch the Addiscombe Cycling Club, a club that still thrives today.

In the years just before looking after Tommy he had achieved great success with managing the mighty trio of Sid Ferris, Charlie Holland and Walter James and in breaking those RRA records. He continued to organise riders on their record attempts into the late 1950s.

Meanwhile Bernard, who was still riding as a professional with the New Hudson / Cyclo gear companies, had the continued support of René Menzies, who was using a motorcycle and sidecar to assist and feed Bernard.

By summer both riders were putting up incredible figures. League tables were being published regularly in the press listing their weekly and up-to-date totals compared with the current record holder's totals for that same period. Tommy reached a peak in June, when on five consecutive days he recorded 258, 295, 361, 291 and 231 miles. The 361 miles covered on June 21 was Tommy's highest daily total. At the end of June Tommy's total for the year was 34,611 miles with Bernard only 717 miles behind. Both riders were well ahead of Ossie's total at that time of the year.

When *Cycling* set up its guidelines and rules for this endurance test in 1910 it did not exclude pacing. Indeed, around that period paced racing was and had been quite common. In June and July 1939 both riders began to pile up massive daily distances by riding with very little or no sleep at all, such was the competition between them and their respective sponsors.

At the end of July, by mutual agreement between the sponsors, a truce was called. Pacing and all other help of an organised kind would be withdrawn and the riders were to be left on their own to continue their individual efforts towards the greatest annual distance by December 31.

Tommy is pictured on one of those long daily rides. He looks uncomfortable on the saddle, perhaps caused by a swollen knee or saddle soreness. *CW*

A huge mileage today means no time for a café stop. A quick snack in Charlie Davey's car has to suffice. *CW*

Tommy is slowed down with busy traffic in Chichester. *CW*

Charlie Davey showing H. H. England (editor of *Cycling*) the sealed
speedometer that is recording Tommy's total mileage. *CW*

Tommy had become a national figure. Sponsored by a famous cycling firm, his face was on posters all over the country advertising drinking some company's beverage and eating another company's breakfast food. He appeared in the BBC programme 'In Town Tonight' and was interviewed several times by Richard Dimbleby; he was the hero of children's comics and met all the leading personalities of the day. The name of Tommy Godwin, in fact, had become synonymous with toughness, rugged determination, mental concentration and endurance.

His exertions in all weathers had made him tough and as hard as a rock. A friend, Frank Edge of the Stone Wheelers Cycling Club, describes him at the time: "He was a remarkable sight. His face and body had been burned a deep mahogany, and his hair and eyebrows had been bleached white." But even Tommy's robust body was not impregnable. He developed a huge swelling on one knee, but ignored his doctor's advice to rest, and the doctor was pleasantly surprised to note a few days later that the swelling had disappeared, despite the fact that Tommy had cycled hundreds of miles since.

As Tommy's daily totals rose, more and more people took an interest in him as he extended his lead over Bernard. Never before in the whole of its history had the year's distance record provided such a sensational story. It had become one of the most dramatic sporting duels cycling had ever seen and the public increasingly were attracted to it.

Although a foolproof system had been devised to check his daily mileage, there were still some doubters. As the *Cycling* publication had been the official scrutineer for this record attempt, their editor H.H. England was invited to make a personal check. Although Tommy had covered 308 miles the previous day, he set out early for Land's End on July 21 and at the end of the day he had completed 348 miles. This was witnessed by the editor, and everyone was satisfied.

This mileage, together with the previous two days' recorded mileage of 333 and 308 miles, gave Tommy the staggering total of 989 miles over 3 consecutive days. He won a prize for this noteworthy achievement. But let us take a look at this a little closer. Tommy was doing an endurance ride, riding every day for a year in all weathers.

The record for the fastest time for completing 1,000 miles at this time was held by Sid Ferris, a fellow Raleigh professional, in a time of 2 days 22 hours 40 minutes. This was a one-off event in racing conditions with no compulsion to ride in the next day or two. Also the weather, including the wind direction, could be chosen, and the record attempt delayed to make conditions more favourable. When you compare the distance that Tommy rode over these three days it was incredible.

His 50,000 miles (80,467 km) so far for the year was recorded on August 29. Raleigh and Sturmey-Archer decided to get as much publicity from Tommy's success as they could. They produced posters and post cards stating this fact. The post card contained Tommy's autographed picture with a description of his achievement to date. They were then distributed to their retailers as giveaways.

When, on September 3, 1939 World War II was declared, disruptions were expected on the roads, with other hazards such as restricted lighting for night riding. The first item to be rationed was petrol on September 16, which could have affected some of the support Tommy was getting at that time. His sponsors decided to send him to Ireland, to avoid disruptions and the petrol rationing to continue his mileage onslaught. Unfortunately the Irish roads did not suit him, un-surfaced, too rough and potholed. After only a few days he returned to England and had decided that riding on familiar roads was a safer bet to continue with his task of beating the record.

Then there was a National Registration day on September 29, when every household in Britain had to fill in a form declaring who was living in their house. Tommy could be described as living at 'no fixed abode' but the government would have devised a system to catch people with this status. Then all residents of the UK were issued with an identity card and a Ration Book. Food was the next to be rationed, but the commencement date had not yet been announced. As Tommy was a vegetarian he was concerned about the quantity of milk, cheese and eggs that was going to be announced for one adult per week. Undeterred, in one fortnight at the end of September he covered more than 3,000 miles (4,828 km). The blackout added to his difficulties, but he took advantage of one or two moonlight nights to bring up his average.

A postman is signing one of Tommy's checking cards. He is witnessing his entry of his day's mileage, place, date, time and signature. *CW*

A Raleigh publicity post card.

This should have been the first of many publicity photos of Tommy. Alas, the outbreak of World War II five days after the date of this card put paid to that.

PRINTED MATTER

The World's Mileage Record
of 62,657½ miles, held by Ossie Nicholson
of Australia, is being attacked by
Tommy Godwin
riding a RALEIGH Bicycle
fitted with
STURMEY-ARCHER 4 speed Hub.
Up to August 29th, 1939, he had covered
the amazing distance of over 50,000 miles.

A good day-time ride, but Tommy and the bike are ready for night-time riding as well. *CW*

After a long day Tommy finds a hair-wash refreshing. Note the candle in his hand ready to wax his hair. *CW*

One of Tommy's regular refreshment stops. *CW*

On a damp, cold morning the time is 10.15 am on Thursday October 26, 1939. The place is Hendon, North London. H.H. England has just signed Tommy's checking card witnessing a figure recorded of 62,658 miles completed. The Australian's previous record is broken with 66 days still to go. *CW*

Celebration by his sponsors at Trafalgar Square. The
'year' record is broken on a cold wet day in London.

Satisfaction is on Tommy's face as the welcoming crowd give him
a cheer on bringing the 'year' record back to Britain.

By October Tommy had considerably increased his lead over Bernard to around 3,500 miles (5,632 km) as he approached the existing record. Charlie Davey had worked out when Tommy would pass the current record distance and set him a route that would lead to a reception in Trafalgar Square, London. The previous day Tommy rode down from Stoke-on-Trent completing a ride of 187 miles at a riding speed of 20 miles per hour, ending up at his digs in Hemel Hempstead. He then prepared himself on this Thursday morning October 26, for a gentle ride to Trafalgar Square and the planned reception. The ride turned out to be far from gentle as it was cold, wet and sleet was falling making conditions far from ideal. The weather reminded Tommy of the day he set out back in January, 299 days ago.

He actually passed Ossie Nicholson's record total of 62,657 miles (100,837 km) at 10.15am on October 26, 1939 at Hendon, North London. Charlie Davey had contacted the editor of *Cycling* to tell him where Tommy would be when the record was broken. So when Tommy arrived in Hendon, H.H. England was waiting for him on this cold, damp, icy morning with a photographer to capture the moment when Tommy and the Editor, both shivering, exchanged signatures on this most important of all the hundreds of checking cards Tommy had been using daily.

He then completed another 14 miles by riding in to Trafalgar Square, London during a brief thunderstorm and slithered off his bike and fell heavily in front of a welcoming crowd. He announced that he was OK, as due to his many falls earlier in the year he had now learned how to fall. Amongst the crowd were representatives of the Raleigh Cycle Company Limited, Sturmey-Archer Gears Limited and the Press. After a photo shoot they went to a nearby hotel where telegrams awaited Tommy which were read out. One from G.H.B. Wilson, Managing Director of Raleigh Cycles said:

Congratulations on covering nearly 63,000 miles on your Raleigh bicycle in 43 weeks, thereby breaking the world's record for year's mileage with nine weeks still to go. A truly wonderful performance on your part and a tribute to British cycle craftsmanship.

Another telegram from R.L. Jones, General Manager of Sturmey-Archer Gears said:

All cyclists will join in congratulating you on your successful attack on world's record for year's mileage. Accept personal congratulations on your great feat in cycling nearly 63,000 miles to date. Your brilliant performance definitely demonstrates that the modern high-grade British bicycle fitted with a four speed hub gear is supreme in quality and dependability.

Addressing the officials and journalists present Tommy said that with blackouts permitting, he hoped to top 75,000 miles (120,697 km) by the end of the year and put the record where it could not easily be beaten. Little did anyone know at the time that Tommy was vastly underplaying his abilities. Maybe he should have said that he was going to make his record impossible to beat. A reporter from a national newspaper then asked how he managed to cope with so little sleep when at times he was riding for 18 or more hours a day. He gave a most amazing answer: "I find that cycling done properly is so restful that I can manage with only five hours sleep a day." He also gave some credit to a small silver horseshoe that he always carried around his neck. Even with the public's distraction of increasingly hostile events taking place all around Europe and beyond, he still managed to receive congratulations from all over the world and his sponsors were certainly ecstatic.

After breaking the year's record Tommy was in demand by the press, the BBC and he had invites to many cycling clubs and their annual dinners, as well as demands from his sponsors to attend various functions. Despite all these distractions, mishaps, weather and visits to hospitals, he only had one day when no mileage was recorded in the entire year of his challenge. That was on October 28, 1939 when his diary entry stated "Day off, Prince of Wales". Although Tommy was teetotal, this must have meant the Prince of Wales pub-restaurant in Drury Lane, Covent Garden in London. It was a regular meeting place of cycling journalists and officials and suffice to say they had invited Tommy to an informal meeting in celebration of his beating of Ossie Nicholson's record two days earlier. Just over a year later the

After interviews with the press Tommy is presented with a hastily prepared but distinctive sweater with his new record of 75,065 miles embroidered on it. He was also presented with a laurel wreath and another handshake from Charlie Davey.

Another surprise for Tommy as Marcel Planes (on the left), the very first 'year' record holder in 1911 congratulates Tommy as the new record holder on December 31, 1939. *CW*

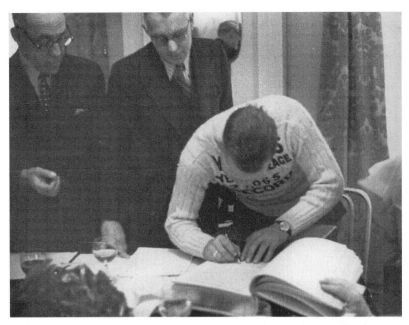

Tommy signing the Golden Book, at the special dinner organised by
Cycling at the Grosvenor House Hotel on New Year's Eve.

Thomas Edward Godwin

The first cyclist to average over 200 miles a day for a year,
'Tommy' Godwin set up a new record for a year's riding between
January 1 and December 31, 1939, by covering 75,065 miles.

The previous best performance was put up in Australia in 1937
by Ossie Nicholson who rode 62,657.6 miles in the year.
Godwin passed this total on October 26, 1939.

Godwin started cycling as a newsagent's delivery boy at the
age of 14 in 1926 and rode his first time-trial, a 25 mile road event,
the same year. Since then he has clocked inside 1 hour 2 minutes
for 25 miles on no fewer than four occasions whilst at the other
end of the scale he has covered 236 miles in 12 hours.

In 1933 Godwin earned the seventh award in the Best All-
rounder Road Riding Competition open to all amateur cyclists
in the United Kingdom with an average speed of 21.255 m.p.h.
His performances were - 50 miles, 2 hrs, 10 mins, 12 secs, 100 miles,
4 hrs, 40 mins, 6 secs, and in 12 hours he covered 231½ miles. He
was then a member of the Potteries C.C.

Club: Rickmansworth C.C.
Age: 27 years
Date: December 31, 1939

Tommy Godwin

Tommy's page in *The Golden
Book of Cycling,* signed at
the celebration dinner at the
Grosvenor House Hotel,
London, held on the evening
of 31 December 1939.

Prince of Wales pub-restaurant became the official headquarters of the newly formed Pedal Club. Amongst its founding members were H.H. England and Charlie Davey.

Tommy was determined to carry on riding every day, but the black-out law was becoming an increasingly severe handicap. This, together with winter approaching, meant that he tried only to ride on familiar roads in the dark.

Bernard Bennett was still riding and on target to beat the Australian's previous record, but when Tommy passed the record on October 26 Bernard was nearly 4,000 miles short of Tommy's total. Also, on that record day in October there were reports of a bombing raid on the Firth of Forth, HMS Southampton being hit and several enemy planes being shot down; these were certainly unsettling times.

On the last day of 1939 Tommy arrived at Trafalgar Square, London and when the clock struck midnight he had covered 75,065 miles (120,805 km) over the previous twelve consecutive months. This set a new world record, beating the previous one by 12,408 miles (19,968 km). He had set a bench mark that even over 70 years later nobody has surpassed. One runs out of superlatives in trying to describe what he had achieved. Tommy had become the first cyclist ever to have averaged a daily mileage of over 200 miles a day for this period. Nobody else has ever achieved such a feat.

Bernard Bennett also beat the Australian's previous record, but finished the year nearly 10,000 miles behind Tommy, achieving a magnificent total of 65,127 miles (104,808 km) at the end of the year.

This outstanding achievement was entered in *The Golden Book of Cycling* at a special dinner organised by *Cycling* at the Grosvenor Hotel, London that night December 31, 1939. This was a day when Tommy recorded one of his lowest distances of the year with only 60 miles. His lowest daily total of 59 miles was recorded on Christmas Day, when he was enjoying time with friends.

Also on that last day of 1939, Tommy's diary was signed off by Charlie Davey and his Nash Mills landlord, Frank Roome.

In the winter of 1939/40 Tommy's bike was equipped with a Dynohub that had to be adjusted so as not to break the black-out laws. At night-time he tried to only use roads that he was familiar with.

6

ON TO ANOTHER RECORD

After breaking the world record and becoming the first rider ever to average over 200 miles a day for a year's riding you would think such an achievement would be enough for anybody. But not Tommy, he was determined to continue riding every day to reach the 100,000 mile (160,930 km) climax. His target was to do it in 500 days. He needed to better the previous best of 532 days set by the Frenchman, René Menzies, in 1938. He had worked out that he 'only' needed to continue at an average of about 185 miles a day to achieve his goal.

It was now a new year, 1940, and World War II was getting serious. The threat of call-up papers for Tommy created some uncertainty as to whether he would be able to complete his 100,000 mile challenge. New Year's day brought reports of a German plane being shot down by the RAF over the North Sea and another German plane was seen heading for the Shetland Isles. Tommy tried to put all this doubt out of his mind while he focused on his task ahead.

Undeterred, Tommy set out on New Year's day with his daily target firmly fixed in his mind, but he recorded only 147 miles. The following day he improved to 190 miles and on January 4 he rode over 200 miles. It was winter, with short days, and there were now wartime restrictions such as strict times for blackouts, and his bike lighting had to be modified to reduce any glare upwards. As there was no other lighting about this meant it was hard for Tommy to see much of the road in front of him. Although he was using a hub dynamo this winter, night riding was problematic. The enemy was sinking ships bringing food to the United Kingdom which caused the government to announce that food rationing was now a certainty and to be expected soon. Finally it was announced that some types of food rationing was to be introduced from January 8, 1940 and this posed an added problem for him to deal with. Three of the first items to be rationed were eggs, cheese and milk, which made up most of Tommy's daily requirements. The details were that each adult would be restricted to three pints of milk, two ounces of cheese and one egg per week.

Tommy needed a lot more than a week's ration for each day's energy requirements. Fortunately, in rural areas milk, eggs and cheese could be obtained without coupons and Tommy's manager, Charlie Davey, also a vegetarian, and with many contacts in rural areas, would be able to obtain most of what Tommy needed on his daily rides. On the downside, Charlie could not be with Tommy 24/7 and when he was using his two main bases to ride from, Stoke-on-Trent and Hemel Hempstead, it was uncertain whether he could get his required intake of food. His landlady at his lodgings in Hemel Hempstead was said to have commented about the great difficulty she had in providing food for Tommy. When he arrived he had an immense appetite after covering the vast distance that he had done that day, and he needed more food to prepare him for riding the following day. The same could be said for his friend's house in Stoke-on-Trent, but fortunately there were a lot of rural areas around the Potteries and other friends would help out. But Tommy carried on undaunted by all these added problems. He showed his true strength and stamina by continuing to ride every day, whatever the weather and however he felt.

After his record-breaking ride in the year previous, he was still in demand by his sponsors and the media. He had to attend a Raleigh dinner on the January 10 to celebrate his new world record. Also visits to the cycling press were required along with other commitments. Then on January 16, winter snow started with a vengeance. At the same time three British submarines were reported missing and US planes began to arrive in England. This was all unsettling news for Tommy, but he was still determined to continue with his quest.

Heavy snow continued to fall for the rest of January and by the end of the month reports of trains and passengers being stranded and villages being cut off were common. Ice and snow was causing havoc to all types of travel. One report in the North Staffordshire Press stated that, "In one day Tommy had skidded and fallen over eighty-four times, surely another world record?" Tommy's diary entry on that day simply said: "109 miles ridden. Bad day. Ice & snow. Roads in very bad condition, but raining heavily." The roads continued to be in a treacherous state, but he was still riding well over 100 miles every day and totalling 5,581 miles for the first month of 1940. It was more than his first month of 1939 and with such precarious roads, this was absolutely amazing!

At one stage during his record rides he fell heavily and damaged a collar bone. He refused hospital treatment and obstinately carried on with an inner tube strapping his arm to his shoulder. He rode one handed until it healed. Who knows, but this, along with his many other falls and injuries sustained, could have had an effect on his later life.

February continued with the atrocious weather. Icy roads, snow and heavy rain did not provide ideal cycling conditions. Several visits to the cycling press and his attendance at the annual Rickmansworth Cycling Club 'Ricky' dinner must have invigorated Tommy as he recorded riding over 200 miles a day on no fewer than ten times in February. But he had to be careful; there were many reports across the country of cyclists and motorists being fined for travelling in the dark on roads with un-obscured lights. The black-out certainly was being enforced.

Winter! It just continued into March, even to the very end of the month, as did his visits to the cycling press and other functions. One day he crashed, smashing his front wheel; another day he had four punctures to deal with. Then, for a bit of variety, he competed in an early season 25-mile time trial in Leicestershire, recording a time of 1 hour 8 minutes and 5 seconds. He was now stepping up his daily mileage to get back on to his schedule; he recorded 200 miles and more for 13 days in March.

At last the weather started to improve in the month of April. There were still more visits to the cycling press, bike repairs and more reports of World War II bombing, all of which served to distract Tommy, but he was determined to complete his task of 100,000 miles in 500 days. Cycling clubs continued to exist and promote events in spite of losing many members to the war services. Tommy rode another 25-mile

Tommy doing a 200 plus mile ride on a cold dry day in March 1940.
The place is Charing in Kent.

Sid Ferris has just handed Tommy a refreshing drink at Hogs Back.

Tommy is riding through Aylesford, Kent, early morning on a cold day in April 1940.

Tommy was a regular visitor to Canterbury. Here he is about to continue on his days ride after a lunch break.

Charlie Davey is handing a drink to Tommy at Abinger Hammer on the A25 between Guilford and Dorking.

Better weather today and Tommy's bike is well prepared for some night riding to keep his daily average on target. *CW*

On another day, Charlie Davey is handing Tommy a drink
after he has ridden 90 miles so far.

Paddington Recreation Ground Track, Whit Monday 13 May 1940.
Tommy starting his final mile on the track to complete his 100,000 miles
and is being pushed off by Billie Dovey.

Paddington Recreation Ground Track, Whit Monday 13 May 1940.
Nearly there! Tommy is approaching the finishing line of 499 days
and 100,000 miles.

Tommy crossing the finishing line. 100,000 miles is now completed.

Charlie Davey, Raleigh's records manager congratulating Tommy on a mission of 100,000 miles completed in 499 days.

This time it is congratulations from H.H. England editor of *Cycling*. Looking on in amazement at Tommy's achievement are two local cyclists.

Paddington Recreation Ground Track, Saturday 18 May 1940. Raleigh put on a special celebration event that was well attended. The picture shows Tommy starting a special lap of honour for his recent 100,000 mile remarkable achievement, being pushed off yet again by Billie Dovey.

Marguerite Wilson presenting Tommy with a laurel wreath at the end of his special lap of honour.

Another lap of honour with left to right, Sid Ferris, Billie Dovey, Marguerite Wilson (part hidden) and Tommy.

The group photo includes from the left, H.H. England, Marguerite Wilson, Sid Ferris, Tommy, Charlie Davey and Billie Dovey.

time trial, this time the Addiscombe Cycling Club event, recording a fast time of 1 hour, 5 minutes and 13 seconds. This private ride was organised by Charlie Davey, who as well as being a joint founder of the club, held an official post with them and was also a registered timekeeper. This ride proved that Tommy had not lost any of his speed, even after piling up such massive mileages. He finished the month of April with less than 2,500 miles short of his target.

Much better weather in May allowed Tommy to enhance his mileage total. Still riding every day he achieved rides of over 200 miles for six consecutive days, including two more visits to the BBC to appear in the 'In Town Tonight' programme, interviewed by Richard Dimbleby (later to become Sir Richard). One of those visits coincided with the announcement of an historic event; Britain had a new Prime Minister – Mr. Winston Churchill.

Tommy's sponsors had worked out when he would reach this magical figure of 100,000 miles. So they planned for Tommy to ride the last mile of his epic journey on the Paddington Recreation Ground Track in London on Whit Monday. 'Billie' Dovey, who had broken several professional women's road records on a tricycle in 1939, was keen to push him off for that final mile. Remember, she was the lady who pinned a twig of heather on him when he started out on January 1, the previous year. Waiting at the finishing line, ready to congratulate him, was H. H. England, editor of *Cycling* and his manager/coach Charlie Davey and other dignitaries.

At the end of that day, May 13, 1940, 499 days after setting out on this incredible journey, Tommy's recorded mileage on his sealed speedometer was showing 100,012 miles. In case of any challenges to his reported daily distances, Tommy continued to ride the next day, recording 167 miles, and then topped it off with a short ride of only 76 miles on the Wednesday. He claimed his record as 500 days to avoid any disputes and this was accepted.

The following Saturday, May 18, at the London Cycling Combine event at the same Paddington track, Raleigh put on a special event to allow Tommy to do a 'Lap of Honour' in front of a large crowd to celebrate his remarkable achievement. Billie Dovey again pushed him off and Marguerite Wilson, who already held several bicycle

Women's Road Records, and then went on to hold all sixteen Women's Professional bicycle records, adorned him with a laurel wreath at the finish. Even though there was a war on, the large crowd present were able to applaud Tommy's heroic world beating performance. Raleigh put on quite a show and was able to have some of their other star riders and officials present at the meeting.

As he was now officially the greatest distance cyclist the world had ever seen, despite wartime restrictions, the Raleigh Company put on a special luncheon in recognition of Tommy's feat at their factory in Nottingham.

7

LIFE AFTER

Tommy had achieved his dream of becoming an endurance record holder twice over. His performance was breathtaking when you consider the margin by which he beat the previous records.

His sponsors were ecstatic about the records that he had achieved them by riding their equipment. Therefore you would expect Tommy to be given a lucrative contract and useful fees from the advertising that followed. Let's face it, these two companies were two of the best well known names in the manufacture of bicycles and equipment in the world in the 1930s.

Fate was to deal Tommy a cruel blow. World War II was beginning to rage. Did Tommy get a Professional bike rider's contact? No, and there never really was a true contract as the initial sponsorship was done in a hurry. The Raleigh and Sturmey-Archer factories were no longer manufacturing the equipment Tommy had used. Their factories were now being used to produce materials for the war effort. Sturmey-Archer was able to do a deal with a Swiss engineering company which produced a hub gear to their design. Although it was imported, it was not sold under the Sturmey-Archer name.

It follows that with no branded production there would be no advertising or fees either. The same could be said for the other equipment suppliers such as Brooks Saddles and Dunlop Tyres. These and other companies were all now involved with war effort production, but that was little comfort for Tommy who had no contract and could claim no advertising fees.

He had been in the saddle for many months and deserved a long, long rest. This he never got. After getting special deferment during his ride, his 'Call-up' papers arrived in May and within three weeks he was in the Army. When he reported for duty the Army soon found out that Tommy could not put his heels on the ground after his epic 500 days in the saddle. As this meant he could not march they sent him to the famous Stoke Mandeville Hospital for treatment to his legs and hands. They soon got him walking and marching properly again, but his hands never fully recovered, staying slightly curled for the rest of his life.

He was then transferred to the RAF and based in the Cheddar area until his demob at the end of the war. Tommy married in 1941 and later brought up a family.

After his discharge from war time service with the RAF, his priority was getting employment to support his family. He was employed for a short time as a chauffeur to the Countess of Norbury, the authoress Faye Ellis. Then a move back to the Potteries beckoned. He settled in the Trent Vale area of Stoke-on-Trent. His first job was that of a bus driver, followed shortly by work at a Dunlop Tyre Company depot in the Etruria area of Stoke-on-Trent. Tommy was reconciled to this by the fact he was working for a company where he had used and relied on its products for the whole of his 100,000 mile endurance feat. He stayed in this employment until the depot closed down. Tommy, along with most of the Dunlop employees, was then transferred to the Michelin Tyre Company in Stoke-on-Trent, which was quite near to his home. This was the last firm that he ever worked for.

When he returned to his home town, instead of rejoining his former club, the Potteries CC, he joined the Stone Wheelers Cycling Club which had a clubroom quite near to where he was living – not that distance was ever a problem to Tommy. This club was founded in 1933 as a touring club but became a racing club later, and many of its members had supported Tommy during his record rides. He had built up a close, friendly relationship with certain members, especially the club's chairman George Hemmings and his wife Edie and Frank Edge and Bill Griffiths.

Once Tommy had settled into full time employment after World War II he wanted to race again, not as a professional but as an amateur. Try as he might, the cycling authorities would not allow this. After his personal attempts had ended in a rejection, a petition, led by Stone

Wheelers, was drawn up by his many friends in the Potteries area, together with many of his friends elsewhere. It was signed by over seven hundred cyclists supporting his request, but it was turned down again on the basis that Tommy and 'Raleigh Cycles' would always be associated with each other even though he no longer had a contract with them.

He was very disappointed about this; he loved cycling and the sport side of it. He then threw himself into coaching club mates at Stone Wheelers Cycling Club and became a mentor and motivator to many riders. He also supported the club in many other ways and could always be relied on to help with the club's social events. On the club's 21st anniversary annual dinner Tommy had a large silk banner with the club's name on it especially made. It was regularly used for many years.

Tommy kept in touch with his friends in his former club, the Rickmansworth CC. He attended their annual dinner for many years, cycling to north London from the Potteries, taking with him several members of Stone Wheelers. In the post-war years the 'Ricky' changed its name to the Harrow and Rickmansworth Cycling Club, mainly for political reasons, and continued to thrive. In 1962 it had about 120 members, but then it started to lose members until it was wound up in the early 1970s.

John Thornhill, now Joint President of Stone Wheelers comments:

Tommy's wealth of knowledge of the cycling world in general, particularly long distance racing together with the short distances, was unparalleled. However, his real passion was for longer distances, he used to reckon that 50 miles upwards were the only distances worth getting your bike out for and that the 25 mile and under were just training rides for the distance events.

His advice on how to ride the distance events was invaluable. For example, in a hundred mile event he would tell you what time he expected you to arrive at a certain point, say 20 to 25 miles from the finish, and if you were still feeling good, then to give it everything you had.

His enthusiasm and encouragement to Stone Wheelers riders competing in time trials was infectious. After a couple of years the club was firmly established as the leading time trial club in North Staffordshire. In 1951 I can remember one local open 25-mile time trial event when Stone Wheelers riders finished first, second, third and took six of the top eight positions. The club also boasted several track riders who were regularly picking up prizes at local events as well as competing around the country.

Tommy was very helpful to the club's riders by arranging for one of his Raleigh friends, who still had strong connections with Raleigh and Sturmey-Archer, to provide some equipment. This friend was none other than Bert James, who set several RRA place-to-place and mileage records in 1937 and 1938 with Raleigh. One record that stood out from the rest was the Hundred Miles in 3 hours 45 minutes and 51 seconds in March 1938, beating the previous record by nearly 10 minutes. Bert was able to supply the club with several wheels with Sturmey-Archer four speed hub gears built into them.

In 1951 the club also attracted a rider from Yorkshire who had secured a job in the Stoke-on-Trent area, the now very well known Jimmy Ogden. He lodged for some time at the family home of the club's three Thornhill brothers.

It follows that a formidable team was put together for the longer distance time trials competing in the well established events in the Birmingham, Manchester and Shropshire areas. He was delighted when in 1952 Stone Wheelers won a team award in the Anfield 100-mile event. Tommy also supported the local Cycling Associations holding several positions in them. He regularly attended the Crewe cycle track where Reg Harris was a frequent rider as an amateur. In 1948 Reg was the current world amateur sprint champion and should have been a gold medal contender for the London Olympics that year but for an injury that prevented him competing. In May of that year Reg was pictured shaking hands with Tommy at the Crewe Track, with the caption 'A meeting of two world champions'. A rider from the Warrington Road Club (Crewe Section), Roy Dixon, was grateful to Tommy when in 1951 riding a 12-hour event in the Midlands, he unexpectedly received support and motivation from him when all the

A meeting of two world champions in May 1948. Reg Harris, Manchester Wheelers and amateur world sprint champion of 1947 shaking hands with Tommy at the Crewe (Cheshire) cycle track.

Reg should have been competing in the London Olympics that year but was unfortunately injured and unable to ride. He turned professional with Raleigh later in the year.

Stone Wheelers Annual Club Dinner 1951.
Tommy's first successful protégé, Eric Thornhill (left) collecting his BAR Trophy from club president Vic Wilshaw, Club Chairman George Hemmings (2nd left), Tommy's former Potteries CC club mate Freddie Brown (5th left), Arthur Stubbs (far right) and Tommy (2nd from right)

North Staffs Roller Contest Final, Victoria Hall, Stoke-on-Trent 1952.
From the left, Jimmy Ogden supported by Tommy, Phil Dorman, Roy
Swinnerton and Arthur Stubbs. All Stone Wheelers riders except for Roy.

Stone Wheelers Annual Club Dinner 1953.
Another Thornhill, John, collecting the clubs Best All Rounder Trophy.
Amongst the group are (from the left) are Club President George
Whittaker, George Hemmings, Bill Griffiths, Frank Edge, Edie
Hemmings, Eric Thornhill, Ken Biddulph, Bert James, Tommy Godwin,
Henry Burton and Rae Thornhill.

Stone Wheelers riders retired early. Apparently Tommy was furious with the Stone Wheelers riders and told them in no uncertain manner.

He also donated several of his trophies to other clubs and was always ready to assist in any way possible in local cycling events. When Stone Wheelers started to promote road races from 1956 onwards, Tommy was keen to volunteer to help and held many official positions in the organising of these events. Club mates can relate many stories about Tommy's involvement in their cycling career. Here are several such stories from John Thornhill (Stone Wheelers' current joint President with his wife Rae) including the story of a bull whip that Tommy used:

My first introduction to Tom was before I became a club member when we lived at Dunkirk Farm [North Staffordshire] in the late forties. My brother Eric was already a Stone Wheeler member and Tom would arrive at the farm at approximately 7.00am to dig Eric out to accompany him for a day out on the bike. This went on for a period of time and each time mother would invite Tom to join us for breakfast. As usual the meal was exceptional because we were blessed with adequate good food through the days of rationing.

It was after one of these breakfasts that my father jokingly presented Tom with an all leather bull whip. You will learn later to see what and when this was put to use!

Each year when the racing handbook was printed we would, at Tommy's insistence, have a meeting to discuss and decide which events we expected to ride. The 'must' rides were the Charlotville 50, Westerly Road Club 100, Anfield 100, Manchester Wheelers 100 and the Manchester Wheelers 12-hour time trials.

These were favourite events that Tommy had ridden and won awards in when he was a very successful amateur in the 1930s. Also they were all clubs where Tommy was well known and had many contacts and friends who could help the Stone Wheelers riders and supporters with accommodation for the night before the early morning starts of events, usually around 6.00am.

John Thornhill continues his stories with:

We had been achieving some respectable times and the next event was a 50-mile time trial at Bingham, Notts. However, the evening prior, brother Eric, Jimmy Ogden and myself visited the local pub and had a couple of pints each, of which Tommy totally disapproved, and the next morning all that he said to us was that he expected good results from all of us.

As normal during the race Tom appeared at different points on the course and checked our times, only to find that we were all riding well down on his expectations. So, he appeared at just a few miles to go and was armed with the leather bull whip with which he gave us several lashes across the back to emphasize disapproval and urge us on! But sadly it was too late; the results were still not what were expected or acceptable to all of us. Therefore, through the rest of the day during the ride home Tommy refused to speak one word to any of us, except he did say it was only what we deserved.

However, at the clubroom on the following Tuesday evening he did not mince his words. Needless to say this did not happen again due to drinking during the racing season.

John also relates some stories about club pranks at Tommy's expense:

We were at Somerford [tea room near Congleton] one Sunday afternoon and our bikes were stacked against an open shed which housed the coal. During our brief stop we decided to empty Tommy's saddlebag of his cape and other items and fill it with as much coal as possible, with the intention of forcing the pace on the ride home and dropping him. But needless to say this did not materialize – he hung, in although he looked rather under pressure, which was so unusual for him. He would just not yield. At the next clubroom meeting he left nothing to the imagination as to what he thought of our sense of humour.

On another occasion, we were returning from the afternoon tea stop at Derby on a Sunday evening. Prior to leaving the café we decided to slightly loosen the seat bolt securing Tommy's seat pillar and then proceeded on our journey waiting for the results of our prank to bear fruit. This did not become apparent until we reached Uttoxeter and from there onwards we just watched the gradual lowering of his saddle and Tommy's knees kept coming out wider and wider, whereupon around Checkley and Blythe Bridge we started to ask him if there was anything wrong with his bike, which he was obviously riding under some difficultly. He adamantly stated that he had no problem and could not understand why we were asking.

Another story from John;

One Sunday afternoon in the late autumn there were approximately twenty members out on the club run riding the back roads from Congleton to Flash in the Peak District. Shortly before arriving there we decided to get off and walk to the tea stop, which was normal to help the weakest riders. Upon parking our bikes Ken Biddulph noticed that one of his crank cotter pins had fallen out and was missing, and nobody had a spare one. Tom took the situation in hand telling us to go inside and have our afternoon tea, which we proceeded to do. Unknown to us Tom had noticed a farm worker's bike leaning by a wall, so he proceeded to 'borrow' one from this bike and replace the cotter pin with a wooden peg. Of course we never heard the outcome but gave that particular tea place a miss for the next few months.

A final story from John:

Tommy was always there to assist all riders who took part in the club's place-to-place events, these being the Stone to Newport, Shropshire and back, Stone to Buxton and back and the Stoke to Banbury and back (using Post offices as the start and turning point).

Finishing one of my rides in the Stoke to Banbury and back attempt, (some 172 miles), I went to Tommy's home and he suggested I took a bath to remove the grit and road dirt, where I promptly fell asleep. After some considerable time Tommy came to investigate, but the door was locked and he had to break down the door before he could awaken me.

I really think he thought I had drowned, but everything was OK except for the door, which was soon repaired. [John was a joiner]

Another story told about Tommy's mischievous ways from Kath Biddulph:

In the early 1950s on a club run on the Staffordshire-Derbyshire border the club was leaving Longnor. As the road climbed severely upwards on the famous hill called Crowdecote the entire club dismounted. As all of us were pushing our bikes up the steepest part of the climb, another cyclist came along and rode past us. It was a female rider and when she was passing Tommy he put his hand out and grabbed her saddle, bringing her to a halt. The air turned blue with the comments she made to Tommy and the rest of us.

In the 1960s he mellowed a little and took up riding a trike. I can remember on a club run in the early sixties where he persuaded me to 'have a go' on it at the Somerford tea room, near Congleton. Never having ridden one before, after a few pedal strokes I ran straight into a garden wall. No damage to the trike, but I still have a small scar on my upper lip where I made contact with the wall.

Eric Thornhill, Tommy, John Thornhill and Mr. Clarke (friend and host). The photo taken by Jim Ogden at the Courtaulds Factory (Preston) Sports Day, Summer 1951. Mr. Clarke was a director and put up the team when they were racing on the Preston (Brock) course events.

8

THE 1971 CHALLENGER

On September 1, 1971 a cyclist named Ken Webb from Sussex set out from Fleet Street in London to challenge Tommy's records. He had contacted Tommy in the months before for advice and he gladly gave Ken Webb some tips. One certain tip that was given was to avoid, at all costs, battling through two winters and to start nearer the middle of the year.

Ken Webb was aged 42 and after 12 years with the Fleet Air Arm had been unemployed for some time. He still had some cash reserves but had little support from any sponsors. By early November his cash reserves were getting low so he took a job at Gatwick Airport, near his home. He planned to keep riding after his work day and during his days off.

To prove his mileage he used a different odometer each month to support the distance shown on the witnessed checking cards he was posting to *Cycling* each day. His accumulative mileage reached Tommy's record total of 75,065 on August 7, 1972. At the end of August his full year's mileage totalled 80,647, which included an extra day as 1972 was a leap year.

His ride was witnessed by fellow Cycling Old-Timer, Dave Rodd of the Catford Cycling Club. He was riding some of the roads being used in the club's 24-hour event in 1972. Later on Dave rode with him during a cycle event held in Southwark Park, North West London, and he told him he was very confident in breaking Tommy's two world records.

He then continued to the end of the year piling up his mileage until, outside Buckingham Palace, he reached his 100,000 miles goal on December 31, 1972 in 448 days. It appeared that both of Tommy's records had finally been broken after a long period of time.

Although Webb had many doubters about his achievements, there were those who thought after thirty-two years, with so many improvements in bicycle equipment and clothing, it was inevitable somebody would beat Tommy's record totals one day. These improvements included lighter aluminium chain wheel, cranks, pedals, wheels and other parts. A greater choice of gear systems gave a choice of ten or more gears compared to Tommy's four. All in all this offered a much lighter bicycle with greater flexibility and reliability. Also a greater knowledge of nutrition was now available and many endurance records were being broken.

The *Guinness Book of Records* acknowledged this new year's distance record and replaced Tommy's entry with Ken Webb's details. The *Cycling* magazine appeared to recognize the new records as well, but it was not scrutinised as thoroughly as the previous records had been.

Friends of Tommy at the Stone Wheelers Cycling Club and others started looking at Webb's claims closely. There appeared to be many areas of his claimed mileage that could be challenged. The distance claimed between two towns or cities was regularly in excess of the actual distance. His answer was that he often went on the scenic route rather than the direct route. A witness was found, and said that they had seen him getting off a train with his bike when he was claiming to have ridden it some large distance that day. Then a real challenge was made to discredit Webb's ride.

The *Guinness Book of Records* accepted this challenge to Webb's claimed distance and removed it from the book, replacing it with Tommy's previous details.

Ken Webb always protested his innocence. He claimed that to obtain the mileage he did not do anything that the previous challengers had done, such as letting someone else ride the bike while catching a few hours sleep, or spinning the wheel while the bike was stationary.

There was, of course, a very big difference between Ken Webb's ride in 1971/2 and that of the two challengers in 1939. Webb's ride was a solo ride, the 1939 challengers, Tommy Godwin and Bernard Bennett, were riding for bicycle manufacturers who were competing with each other to claim this endurance prize. The members of the support teams would have been watching each other like hawks and if there was any suspect mileage being recorded, they would have immediately challenged it.

Webb never had this scrutiny during his ride. He argued that the factory-sealed odometers he sent in to the magazine were proof enough that his claimed mileage was correct. But there were just too many flaws in his claims for his record to be ratified as a serious claim.

9

FAREWELL TOMMY

Tommy made a wonderful gesture to his close friends George and Edie Hemmings by gifting them his very large collection of photographs taken during his record rides. He then presented his diaries for the relevant two years to their son Neil for safe keeping.

In the early 1970s Tommy was again very active in supporting and encouraging riders in local cycle events. He also continued to hold official posts in various cycle clubs and associations. He enjoyed cycling at all levels and was still a regular on the Stone Wheelers Cycling Club weekend club runs.

On a Sunday in July 1975 when returning from a day out cycling with friends, including George and Edie, and only a mile away from his home, Tommy died suddenly of a heart attack. He was 63.

At his funeral on August 3, as well as family members and close friends attending, there were representatives of the following: Stone Wheelers Cycling Club, North Staffs Cyclists Track Association, BCF North Staffs Centre, Stoke-on-Trent City Cycling & Athletic Club, Tunstall Wheelers, Leek Cycling Club, Janus Road Club, Manchester Wheelers, Dukinfield Cycling Club, Velo Club Ventroux (Stafford), Congleton Cycling Club, Youth Hostels Association, The Cyclists Touring Club and Veterans Time Trials Association. The world of cycling paid tribute to one of the sport's most illustrious figures and a remarkable athlete.

The day he died the cycling world lost one of its great heroes, Stone Wheelers Cycling Club lost a great supporter and motivator, his family lost a great husband, father and grandfather, and many lost a great friend. It was often wondered if his early demise was due to the gigantic effort required or the many tumbles he suffered during his record rides.

Anyone who witnessed his record ride could never forget it and anyone who knew him could never forget him. Unlike some athletes who reach the top and then leave their sport, Tommy remained and ploughed back his expertise and experience. The memories of Tommy lingered on locally, with his friends and all the people who had made contact with him over the years. But as the years passed, these memories faded and many younger people would not know of his achievements. Other than memories and some old press cuttings, there was nothing to remember him by, no book, no plaque, just stories that got passed down and got a little distorted over time.

In July 2004, a local journalist ran a well written and illustrated feature in a North Staffordshire newspaper in the series 'All Our Yesterdays' on cycling in the 1960s and 1970s. There was no mention of Tommy Godwin, and this, unknowingly, sowed the seed for a new interest in Tommy's performances.

A local cyclist, Ivan Dix, sent in a letter to the newspaper congratulating the journalist for his excellent article and saying how much he had enjoyed it, as cycling rarely receives any recognition. He then went on to say that it had brought to mind the fantastic achievement of the Potteries cyclist Tommy Godwin of Trent Vale in 1939 and 1940. Then he posed the question, "Is there anything to commemorate it?" and went on to suggest some methods to do so.

Amazingly, although the suggestion had been made by his friends many times before, to no avail, this time it struck a cord and created a lot of interest. Several letters were then received by the newspaper agreeing with the idea.

By the month of October that same year a campaign was started in earnest. One of his daughters had contacted the Mayor of Stoke-on-Trent, Mike Wolfe, who liked the idea. A local company offered to make and supply, free of charge, a suitable plaque and the Mayor obtained permission for it to be placed in a local sports centre.

It followed that on Monday March 14, 2005 a commemorative celebration was held at the Fenton Manor Sports Centre in Stoke-on-Trent. The Mayor addressed a large group of cyclists and said that we should remember someone with boundless energy and who was a real role model. Tommy aimed for the top and is still well remembered in many parts of the world. Then he introduced ninety year old Edie Hemmings, Stone Wheelers' current President, who, with her late husband George, had been very close friends of Tommy for many years. Edie then unveiled the plaque to much applause from the audience. The plaque was inscribed as follows:

THIS PLAQUE
COMMEMORATES THE OUTSTANDING ACHIEVEMENT OF
STOKE-ON-TRENT CYCLIST

TOMMY
GODWIN

HOLDER OF THE WORLD MILEAGE ENDURANCE RECORD
OVER THE TWELVE MONTHS OF 1939 (75,065 MILES)
AND THEN WENT ON TO CYCLE 100,000 MILES IN 500 DAYS

THIS ACHIEVEMENT IS UNSURPASSED AND HAS
BEEN RECOGNISED BY
THE GUINESS BOOK OF RECORDS
AND WILL REMAIN TOMMY'S RECORD IN PERPETUITY
HIS NAME IS ALSO ENTERED IN
THE GOLDEN BOOK OF CYCLING

PLAQUE DONATED BY MOULDART LIMITED
FOR THE FAMILY OF TOMMY GODWIN
AND FOR THE PEOPLE OF STOKE-ON-TRENT

After that the Mayor introduced another Potteries top cyclist, Phil Griffiths, who told the assembled audience that his father, Bill, was a friend of Tommy's and related some stories that his father had told him about the long rides that they used to do together. He went on to give us his memories of Tommy when he himself was a young man. A description he gave of Tommy was that "he was a hard man with a soft touch. He had a lot but he gave it all away. He got so much pleasure from it."

When this ceremony took place it was nearly sixty-five years after Tommy had completed his remarkable ride. But there is a saying that goes; 'Better late than never', and in this instance there could not be a better saying.

A final tribute to Tommy from John Thornhill:

Tommy touched so many lives in the cycling world at large and his world record was known and admired throughout the world. However, to his own club, Stone Wheelers, he was such an inspiration to all and was respected both as a man and a Great, Great Cyclist."

It is a fact that Tommy was the greatest long distance cyclist the world has ever seen. His feat must rank as one the greatest endurance achievements ever attained by a human being.

Fenton Manor Sports Complex, Stoke-on-Trent

*The plaque was mounted on a column at the entrance
to the Sports Complex during a commemorative
celebration on 14 March 2005.
(See Chapter 9)*

Thomas Edward Godwin

The first cyclist to average over 200 miles a day for a year, 'Tommy' Godwin set up a new record for a year's riding between January 1 and December 31, 1939, by covering 75,065 miles.

The previous best performance was put up in Australia in 1937 by Ossie Nicholson who rode 62,657.6 miles in the year. Godwin passed this total on October 26, 1939.

Godwin started cycling as a newsagent's delivery boy at the age of 14 in 1926 and rode his first time-trial, a 25 mile road event, the same year. Since then he has clocked inside 1 hour 2 minutes for 25 miles on no fewer than four occasions whilst at the other end of the scale he has covered 236 miles in 12 hours.

In 1933 Godwin earned the seventh award in the Best All-rounder Road Riding Competition open to all amateur cyclists in the United Kingdom with an average speed of 21.255 m.p.h. His performances were :- 50 miles, 2 hrs, 10 mins, 12 secs, 100 miles, 4 hrs, 40 mins, 6 secs, and in 12 hours he covered 231⅝ miles. He was then a member of the Potteries C.C.

Club: Rickmansworth C.C.
Age: 27 years.
Date: December 31, 1939

Tommy Godwin

Index of Names and Places

 **Stone Wheelers
Cycling Club**

Stone Wheelers is one of the oldest Cycling Clubs in North Staffordshire and celebrates its 80th anniversary in 2012.

The club is based in Stone and has a current membership of 60 from Central and North Staffordshire.

Currently the clubroom is at Stone Tennis Club, Newcastle Road, Stone, ST15 8LD and meets Thursday evenings @ 8pm throughout the year

The club promotes a wide range of training rides, club runs, tutorials and social events.

Also the club regularly promotes road racing and time trial events throughout the season.

For more up-to-date information on the above and membership details please visit our website:

www.stone-wheelers.co.uk

RoadPeace

RoadPeace is the national member-based UK charity providing support for victims of road crashes and campaigning for justice and road danger reduction.

Our Vision

RoadPeace's vision is for a world in which the lives of those killed and injured on the road are no longer treated by the economy as expendable, by the judicial system as trivial and by society as accidents, and in which road crash victims receive the same rights as other victims of crime.

Our Mission

Our aim is to support and empower road traffic victims, to improve the post--crash response they receive, and spare future generations from preventable death and injury.

Our work includes:

- Reducing the suffering of road crash victims by providing practical information and advocacy, as well as emotional support.
- Campaigning for an effective post-crash response, in particular improved investigation, prosecution, compensation and care.
- Representing the interests of road crash victims in their fight against criminal, civil and social injustice.
- Campaigning for road danger reduction and safer streets through tackling criminal and anti-social driving and promoting sustainable transport.
- Increasing awareness of the devastation resulting from road deaths and injuries, using research, testimonies and acts of remembrance.

Our support services include a helpline and befriender network, a six week Resilience Building programme, on-line discussion forum and guides on the legal procedures that follow a road crash.

Founded on the principle of road danger reduction, RoadPeace promotes policies which give greater consideration to vulnerable road users and the environment. This includes two main campaigns:

See Me Save Me, which seeks to reduce the threat to cyclists and pedestrians posed by HGVs;

and

Speed Matters, aimed at raising awareness of the burden imposed on society by excessive and inappropriate speed.

Contact details

www.roadpeace.org

helpline (for victims):   0845 4500 355

office: 020 7733 1603

Unit F6, Shakespeare Business Centre,

245a Coldharbour Lane,

London SW9 8RR

Registered charity 1087192, charitable company limited by guarantee 4165519

To donate to RoadPeace, please go to http://www.roadpeace.org/donate/index.html or http://www.justgiving.com/roadpeace

John Wood membership secretary

Fellowship of Cycling Old-Timers

56 Chestnut Avenue, Eastleigh, SO50 5AL

☎: 02380613280 🖥: johnpen@sky.com

The FCOT publishes a quarterly magazine, *Fellowship News*, in which members are able to reminisce over past events, give and seek news of old friends and acquaintances, discuss current facts and fancies, and generally air their memories, their opinions, their hopes and their fears on any subjects they care to raise, cycling or non-cycling. Editing of letters is done only with the writers' consent - there is no censorship.

BINDON ABBEY MILL.
*where Angel Clare proposed to learn milling.
Tess of the D'Urbervilles.*

The magazine is A5 size and contains illustrations (including sketches by Frank Patterson, the artist who captured the spirit of cycling better than anyone else, by kind permission of the CTC and Temple Press). It is printed by offset litho, and usually has 100 pages, or more.

The FCOT is not intended to be an active body competing with the CTC, the VTTA the Autumn Tints Cycling Comrades or any other national or local associations, but that does not mean that active cyclists are not welcome. They are often keenly interested in the past, and are glad to refresh their memories of people and events and to say what they are thinking. In fact most COTs are still active; many of them assert that in *Fellowship News* they have a paper which embodies the essence of cycling to an extent unequalled by any other magazine today.

APPLICATION FORMS FOR NEW MEMBERS I can send you forms either by post or email (in Adobe Reader format that you can print out as often as you like) so that you can give them to prospective members.